TURTLES

Written and Illustrated

by WILFRID S. BRONSON

HARCOURT, BRACE & WORLD, INC., NEW YORK

TURTLES

There are turtles in many different countries, but this book is nearly all about American turtles. Most turtles live in water, but some live on land. Land turtles are called tortoises.

A turtle is one kind of reptile.
Other kinds of reptiles are
snakes, lizards, crocodiles, and

alligators. All reptiles have scaly
bodies. But, unlike the scaly
fishes, their skins are not slimy,
and they breathe air, not water.
Like fishes and frogs, reptiles

are cold-blooded. When weather
turns cold, their blood grows
cold too. This makes them slow
and sleepy, so they sleep. Birds
and the mammals (animals that
have milk for their babies — like
cows, cats, dogs, and people),
are warm-blooded. Except for a
few kinds, like bears and wood-

chucks, cold weather makes
their hearts beat faster, not
slower. They move more quickly
and keep warm and wide
awake. Wherever winters are
cold, snakes and lizards, turtles
and tortoises, go to bed till
spring. Turtles sleep in mud be-
neath the water; snakes, lizards,

and tortoises, in the ground.
A crocodile looks like a giant
lizard. A snake is like a lizard
without legs and eyelids. A
turtle is like a lizard plus a shell.

The box-like shell is made of the turtle's own wide ribs inside and big scales outside, all grown together. The scales are made of a stuff like fingernails.

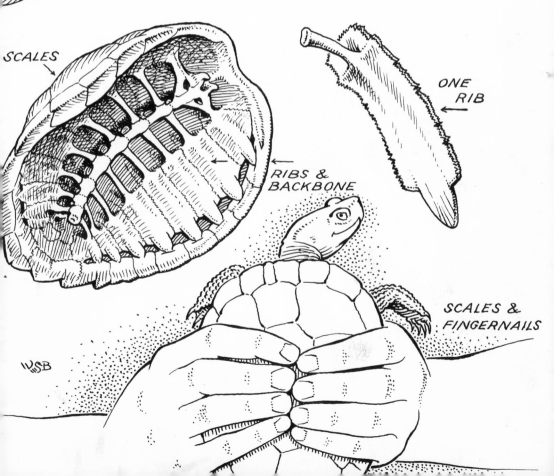

SCALES

ONE RIB

RIBS & BACKBONE

SCALES & FINGERNAILS

The shell is thick and very strong. It is like a bridge. The arched bridge does not break under heavy traffic. The arched shell does not break even in the jaws of a big dog.

The bottom of the shell is not arched but flat, so that the turtle's legs can reach the ground. A turtle crawls along in its heavy shell much like a creeping baby.

The turtle hisses and pulls its
head and legs and tail into its
safe shell when it is afraid of
anything, like a big wild bird
or animal, or your dog or cat,
or you.

Some other animals hiss (snakes, geese, owls), but only a turtle

can hide inside itself. Inside the shell, a turtle's neck folds up like a letter S. When all seems safe, the head comes slowly out again.

THIS PLAN SHOWS HOW THE NECK FOLDS UP LIKE AN S

If the turtle is not scared but

angry, it can shoot its head out
like lightning and bite with its

strong jaws. There are no teeth on the jaws, but the edges are as hard and sharp as the beak of a bird. They cut like curving scissors.

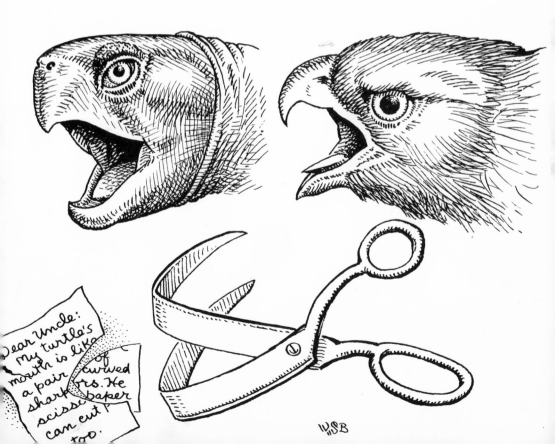

THE
ONLY
SAFE WAY
TO PICK U
A SNAPPIN
TURTLE ~

There are many kinds of turtles, some good-natured, some very bad. The fiercest biters of all are the snapping turtles. They do not try to hide in their shells (which are too small anyway), but snap angrily in all directions, even over their backs. They can bite a stout broomstick in two or take off your fingers in one quick chop!

A snapper swims up under a
duck and pulls it under water
for a meal as easily as you pick

berries from a bush. Or it may lie on the bottom with mouth wide open, twirling its tongue like a worm till a foolish fish swims in to eat the "worm" and gets eaten instead.

Musk and mud turtles also

have bad tempers, and a bad smell. They bother fishermen by taking the bait. Mud turtles have their bottom shells hinged to close up very tightly.

A MUSK TURTLE

The peevish pancake turtle's shell is not hard and bony, but

tough and leathery. This turtle hardly ever leaves the water, but when it does it goes back before its shell gets dry. If it needs more air while sleeping

in the bottom mud, it just stretches up its long neck and pokes out its funny snout to breathe.

The great turtles that live in the

HAWKSBILL,

LEATHERBACK,

sea have very sweet tempers.
They never try to bite when
they are caught. Their front
feet are not like fresh-water
pond turtles'. They are shaped
like paddles and used almost
like wings for "flying" through

GGER-
HEAD,

AND
GREEN
TURTLE

the water. They may be folded over their backs like a bird's wings when sea turtles sleep.

A BABY SEA TURTLE SLEEPING ON SEAWEED

A GARTER SNAKE FAMILY

"We hatched before—"

All reptiles hatch from eggs. With some kinds the eggs are laid first and then hatch. But with others the eggs hatch before they are laid and then the little ones are born. This is the way with many kinds of snakes. But all turtles hatch from eggs after they are laid, like birds.

I'm hatching a long time after~
BABY SNAPPING TURTLE
BABY HAWK
too~

A PAINTED POND TURTLE *lays her eggs~*

1

2

If you
could
see
down
into
the
dirt

In early summer the mother turtle digs a hole in soft dirt or sand. She uses her hind feet, sinking backward as she digs. When the eggs are laid she covers them with earth and leaves them for the warm sun to hatch.

As soon as the baby turtles
hatch they hurry toward the
water. There they will feel safer

from their enemies. Their shells are still soft, and animals like crows and gulls and foxes and wildcats can eat them easily. Or men may catch them to sell in pet stores.

In the water the little turtles feed on tadpoles and snails and worms and insects. They grow fast and each scale of the shell adds a wide new rim every summer. By counting the rims you can tell how old a growing turtle is.

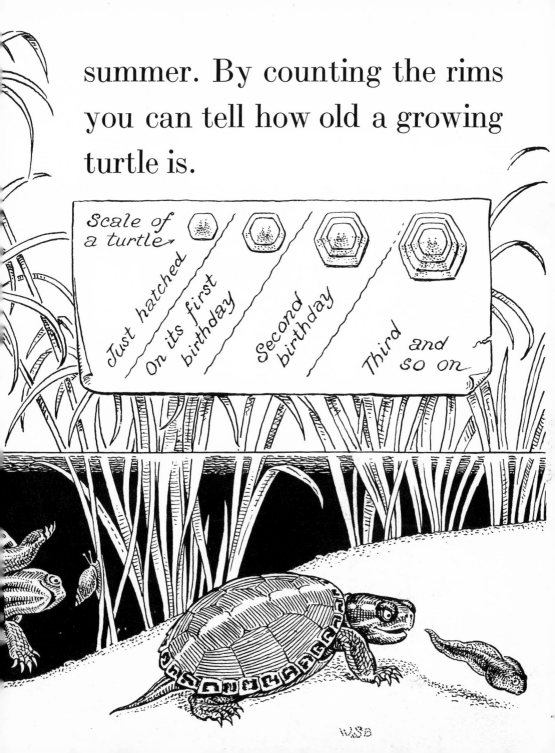

Scale of a turtle →

Just hatched

On its first birthday

Second birthday

Third and so on

Grown-up turtles' scales add hardly any rims. The scales of very old turtles may be smooth, the scale rims worn away. All painted turtles shed the surface of their scales. So no rims are formed that you can count. You can only guess the age. But they live at least as long as we do.

Many have scars on their shells. Notice any scars on the next turtle you meet and you may meet it year after year. Most turtles do not wander far from home.

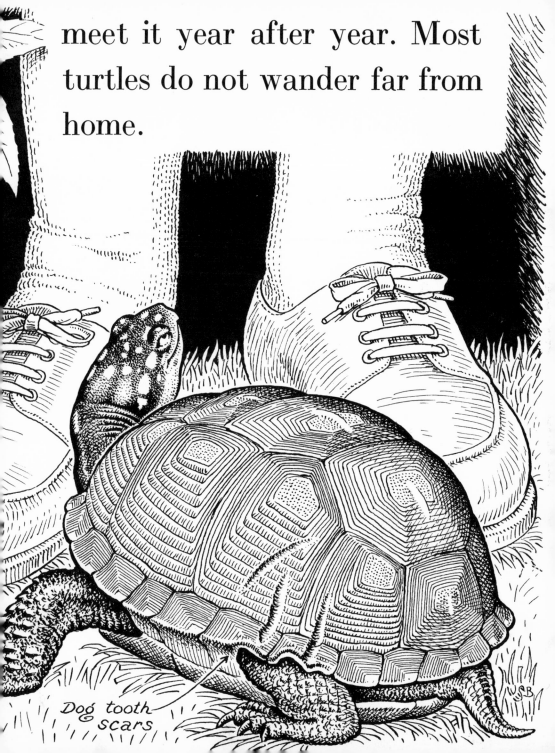

Dog tooth scars

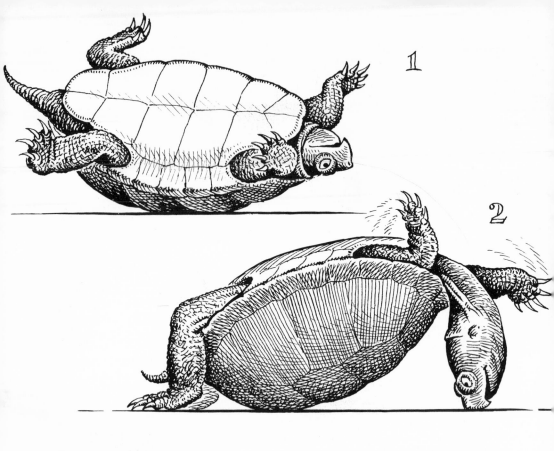

If you turn your turtle friend upon its back, it uses its long neck to lift its forward end, and flips itself right side up with its feet.

Turtles like it in the water. They

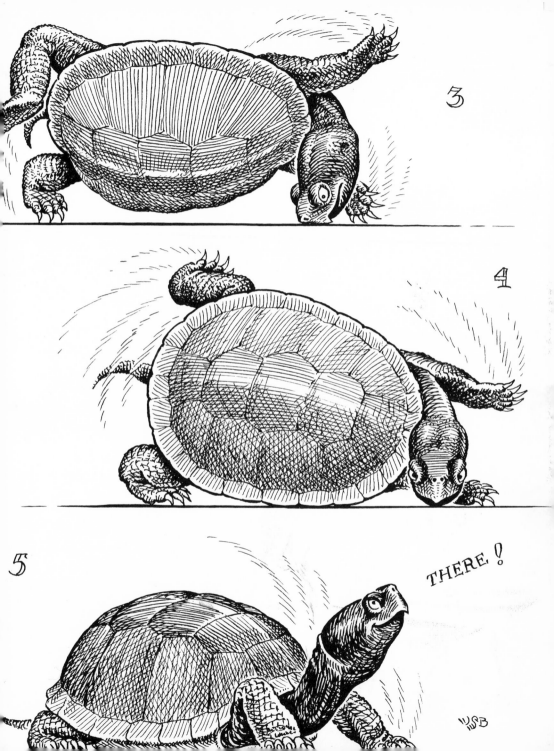

also like to dry off in the sun.
Turtles are deaf but they watch
for danger with their keen eyes.
If one sees you suddenly and

dives from the old log, where
they sun themselves, all dive
after him and swim down out
of sight.

They wabble at first, their wide
webbed feet are such big paddles. But they go faster and
more smoothly and soon hide.

They can hold their breath
for a long time under water. At
last their heads bob up and
soon they climb the log again.

Why do turtles swallow so often?
Take a big breath and hold
your ribs. Feel how they stretch
and help suck in the air. A turtle's ribs, part of the stiff shell,
cannot do that. So it pumps
air in by swallowing. For the
same reason it needs extra loose
skin on its neck and legs, be-
cause the stiff, tight shell will
not stretch when the turtle
moves. Male turtle shells are a
little "hollow-chested"; male
tails are longer than female tails.

My nose and eyes are so close together I can breathe and see without showing much of myself above the water.

A SWALLOW OF AIR ~ IN THE LUNGS

IS LIKE ~

THIS!

MALE AND ♂

FEMALE ♀

Turtles eat under water. They
steal slowly toward their prey,
then suddenly snap. But they
will speed after tadpoles that
are swimming. If the food is

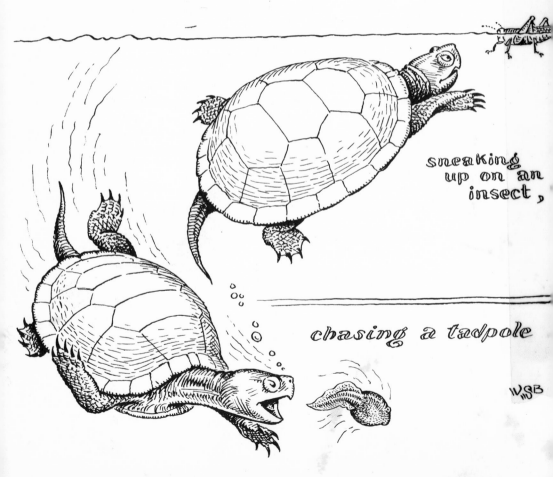

sneaking
up on an
insect,

chasing a tadpole

WSB

too much to swallow whole,
they tear it with their claws.
This also combs it out straight

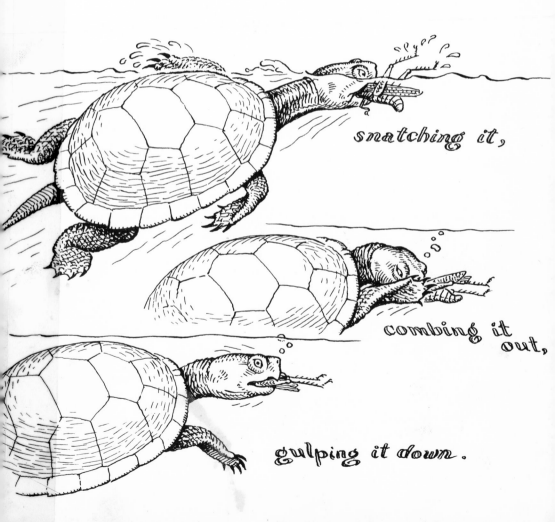

snatching it,

combing it out,

gulping it down.

and aims it down their throats.
There are some kinds of turtles
that will drink water, but they
stay on land and eat vegetables.
They are called tortoises, and

DO NOT DISTURB
Sleeping Hours:
9:30 A.M. to 6:30 P.M. in
Summer & All the time
from Fall to Spring.
Signed, A. Tortoise

they make good pets. They never bite, and soon learn to eat from your hand. The shell of a tortoise is high and its tail is short. It has no webs between its toes, and its claws are dull from walking on land and digging burrows. There it sleeps when winds are wet and cold, or the sun is too hot.

In zoos you may see giant tortoises which can carry children on their backs. They come from

islands west of South America, in the Pacific Ocean. There they make no burrows but wander about eating cactus, spines and

all. Here in our zoos they enjoy good North American vegetables. They grow fast on these, as you can see from the wide pale rims on their scales.

Box "Tortoise"

A few American tortoises, or turtles, don't seem to know which they are, nor care. They act like both. Some have stubby tortoise feet, but others have webs between their toes. Box turtles have short tails and high shells like tortoises, but the bottom of the shell is hinged like a mud turtle's. Both box turtles and wood turtles go into the water, but also wander for weeks ashore. They eat both animals and vegetables, under water or out of it.

I MAY BE A TURTLE, BUT I GUESS I WILL GO ASHORE FOR A MONTH OR SO.

Wood "Turtle"

You never can make pets of snapping, pancake, musk, or mud turtles. But the many other kinds of pond turtles will be more friendly. In cities you can buy baby turtles and keep them in an aquarium. Do not

buy "ant eggs" to feed them. Buy turtle food, or give them little bits of raw meat and fish and lettuce leaves. Take out all they do not eat, each time you feed them. Once a day is plenty. Give them both shade and sunshine and a raft where they can dry themselves. If they have paint on their backs, peel it off gently with a penknife. It is bad for them.

ROCK ISLAND FOR BABY TURTLES

A ...SH~ ...SIN ...ND WITH A

Better still, if you have a yard,
keep your turtles, big or little,
in a pen with a water basin big
enough to swim in, sunk to its
rim in the ground. Give them
a hiding place ashore and some
soft dirt for egg-laying if it is
springtime. Never keep turtles

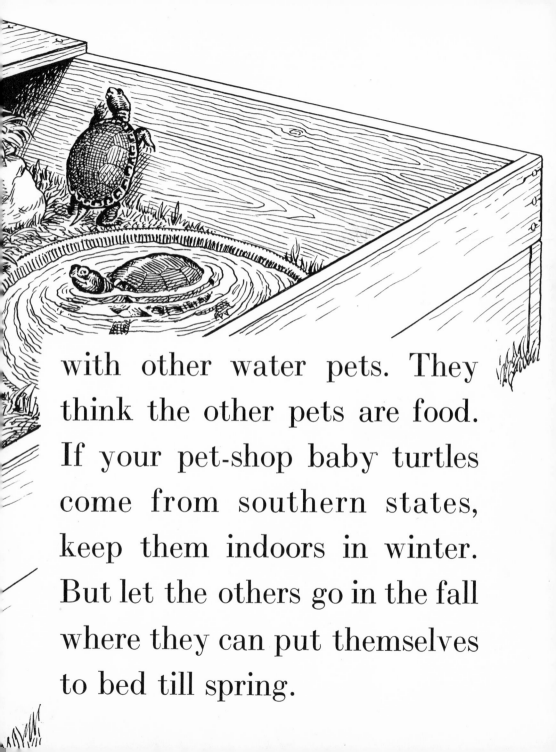

with other water pets. They
think the other pets are food.
If your pet-shop baby turtles
come from southern states,
keep them indoors in winter.
But let the others go in the fall
where they can put themselves
to bed till spring.

So much for tortoises and turtles. But what is a terrapin? Any turtle or tortoise a cook may hope to use for soup, is a terrapin. When people begin to talk of terrapins, it is time for turtles to say

GOODBYE!

THE END